Perhaps at no other time in history has our noble profession been more challenged. Throughout our great nation and within the Golden State, questions about the role we all have in maintaining a just and peaceful society are at the forefront of public discussion. Such scrutiny about our methods, and even our intentions, tends to foster a sense of uneasiness or uncertainty.

Against this backdrop is the powerful reality of your service, as you take up the call each day, to serve the public with distinction and honor, and without fear, favor, or discrimination. Few individuals possess the willingness to put their lives on the line for the greater good. Fewer still have what it takes to wear the uniform of the California Highway Patrol.

Your acts of kindness, compassion, and bravery are routine and often go unnoticed by the public we serve. You are motivated by a sense of duty rather than a need to receive praise. Such selfless acts are the hallmark of our profession and the basis for the public's support of our mission.

We must never forget our heritage, nor squander the opportunities we have each day as public servants to make a positive difference in our society. As we build upon the reputation established by our predecessors, always remember what it took to earn your badge and what it means to wear it each day. Providing the highest level of Safety, Service, and Security to the public is not only our mission—

it is our privilege.

 FranklinCovey.

FranklinCovey
2200 West Parkway Blvd.
Salt Lake City, UT 84119

ISBN-13: 978-1-933976-77-8

GOV151705 Version 1.0.3

With special gratitude to Shawn Moon, Preston Luke,
and the FranklinCovey Law Enforcement Team

NOBILITY *The* OF POLICING

GUARDIANS OF DEMOCRACY

"The wicked flee when no man pursueth:
but the righteous are bold as a lion."

Proverbs 28:1

This book is dedicated to the honorable men and women who serve and protect our communities each and every day; to those who have sacrificed their lives, for us, in the line of duty. Words cannot express our boundless gratitude to those who honor the nobility of policing.

The NOBILITY OF POLICING

2

foreword

> **"It has always been my firm belief that** policing is one of the most noble professions.
>
> # The actions
> ## of any police officer,
> **in an instant, can impact an individual for life,**
>
> **and even a community for generations. Given this realization,**
>
> every police officer must be centered on what is important.
> Service, justice, and fundamental fairness—these are the foundational
> principles in which every police action must be grounded.
>
> *The nobility of policing demands the noblest of character."*
>
> Dr. Stephen R. Covey

THIS BOOK WAS WRITTEN TO

HONOR & SERVE YOU.

Let it serve as a reminder of why policing became your chosen calling. As an inspiration to reignite what might be a waning passion. As renewed awareness and understanding of the nobility of policing, and how critical policing is to the quality of life of the communities and people you serve.

Let it speak to you of the things you may already know to be true, but are too easily forgotten and lost in the chaos of a world that is often ungrateful, unforgiving, and filled with too much pain.

In times of great challenge, there is no greater need than for the nobility of policing to nurture and protect democracy.

KEEP A VISUAL ON THE RESIDENCE, OF
ON THE S/E CORNER OF THE RESIDENCE ITS
CORP. AND OFC. COMPLETED ON

The strength of a democracy

and the quality of life enjoyed by its citizens

are determined in large measure by the ability of the police

to discharge their duties. If we think what we do on the front lines doesn't

affect the quality of life of all those in the community, we need to wake up

and understand the impact of what we do every day."

Herman Goldstein

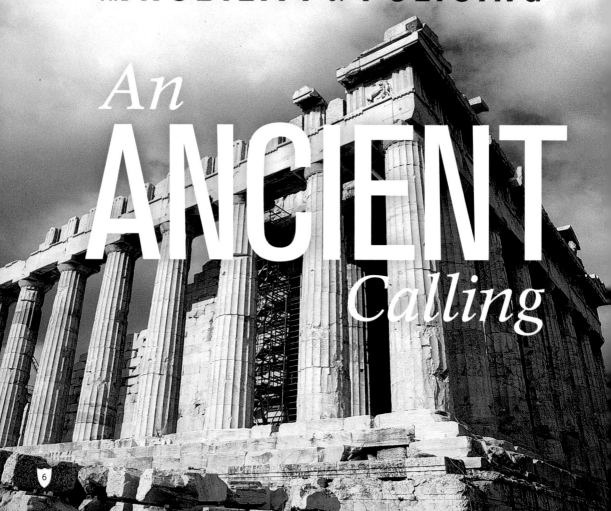

THE **NOBILITY** OF **POLICING**

An

ANCIENT

Calling

6

What is nobility?

no•bil•i•ty |nōˈbilədˌē|
Nobility is greatness of character and high ethical qualities
or ideals that serve a cause greater than self; faithfulness
to a higher calling or purpose.

Thousands of years before the policing profession was established, it had a name. In Plato's vision of the perfect society—a republic that honors the core of democracy—**the greatest amount of power was given to those he called the Guardians.** Only those with the most impeccable character would be chosen to bear the responsibility of protecting the democracy. These Guardians would love the community more than anything else, and never act in any way to harm it. They would be entrusted to preserve its ideals, the sanctity of human dignity, and life itself.

In the words of Plato:

"It does not matter if the cobblers and the masons fail to do their jobs well, but if the Guardians fail, the democracy will crumble."

As guardians of the longest-running democracy in the history of the world, you cannot fail—you dare not fail—to honor the call. The risk is far too great and the margins for error far too slim!

Fighting   604 20th Avenue.   RECEIVED
Nature and Location   MAR 2 6 1984

Every officer is a
LEADER,

"To every man there comes in his lifetime that special moment when he is figuratively tapped on the shoulder and offered a choice to do a very special thing, unique to him and fitted to his talents. What a tragedy if that moment finds him unprepared or unqualified for the work which will be his finest hour."

Sir Winston Churchill

and a

LEADER

always represents *hope.*

Police officers are both blessed and cursed to see more of life in a year than most people will see in a lifetime. The challenge and uncertainty of policing requires the discipline of constant readiness. As a "peaceful warrior," you must always be prepared—mentally, physically, emotionally, and spiritually—for those moments when you are tapped on the shoulder and thrust into circumstances that are beyond imagination.

Rel. Info

Officer Anthony (Tony) Pedeferri spent the beginning of his career learning the job. He stopped road cycling and exercising, which resulted in him gaining 60 pounds. Despite no competitive experience with running or swimming, he turned towards triathlons to remedy his weight gain. Barely surviving his first triathlon, this called into question his declaration to one day compete in an Ironman. Officer Pedeferri trained rigorously

and improved, successfully completing 10 Ironman competitions, including three trips to the World Championships in Hawaii. At the time, the sport was an enjoyable and healthy lifestyle, but he had no idea it would one day save his life.

On December 19, 2007, while Officer Pedeferri was on a traffic stop, a 20-year-old driver approached his location at a high rate of speed. The driver veered off the road and collided into the SUV Tony had stopped. The impact forcefully pushed the SUV into Officer Pedeferri, who was knocked out of his boots and propelled nearly 100 feet into a ditch along the roadway. He was located by rescuers who could not detect a pulse or respirations. He was immediately rushed to the ER, and despite the initial prognosis of only having 10 minutes to live, Tony survived! Though he survived his critical injuries, Tony was paralyzed from the chest down.

Through Tony's perseverance, drive, and determination, he began racing competitively in hand cycling in 2010. Tony went on to win several races, including multiple national championships. In 2012, he was one of four hand cycle athletes named to the 2012 U.S. Paralympic team to compete in London.

In Tony's own words, "I lived a full life and enjoyed it immensely prior to the accident, and I have no regrets. My new life is drastically different, but no less fulfilling." Tony's life has challenges that he is always ready to face and tackle head on.

Tony encourages everyone to step outside their normal comfort zone by experiencing things they thought were too difficult. He is regarded as a hero and continues to be an inspiration for CHP cadets and officers alike.

Are you ready?

0741

11

POLICING
DEMANDS
NOBILITY

"No one is compelled to choose the profession of a police officer; but having chosen it, *everyone* is obligated to perform its duties and live up to the

high standards

of its requirements."

President Calvin Coolidge

To whom much is given, much is required. From the moment the badge is entrusted to you, you commit to serving the greater good **in a spirit of service, justice, and fundamental fairness.** You will perform countless acts throughout your career—some may have profound impact, while others are simply acts of kindness and compassion. The focus of those actions, great or small, must remain centered on serving a noble cause. This deeper meaning and purpose for why policing exists is the strength that will steel you from the ever-present forces of doubt. It is the fuel that will ignite a passion to make a difference—within yourself, to the countless lives you touch, and to the communities you protect on the front lines of democracy.

After losing two police officers in the line of duty, a police chief once remarked:

"What our officers did yesterday was not their most heroic act. The day they embraced this profession, when they committed to a cause and willingly accepted a life of risk and uncertainty to serve a cause, was their most heroic act! Every day after that was simply in the line of duty."

NOBLE ATTITUDE:
THE BATTLE OF THE BULGE

I t is December 1944, the Battle of the Bulge in the Ardennes Forest. The German SS troops have broken through the American lines. The American troops are in retreat, fleeing through the forest in disarray. The 82nd Airborne is dispatched to the forest with three missions: stop the retreat of the American troops, organize them to hold the line, and stop the advance of the German troops. The 82nd Airborne hikes two days to get to the forest.

Now picture this:

An American tank, 30 tons of death, fleeing down one of the little roads leading through the forest. One lonely paratrooper stands beside the road— a young man with hollow, sunken eyes, a three-day growth of beard, an M-1 Garand in one hand, and a bazooka slung over his back. He raises his hand to stop the fleeing tank. After it grinds to a halt, the weary paratrooper looks up at the tank commander and asks:

"Hey buddy, are you looking for a safe place?"

"Yeah," the tank commander replies.

"Then park your tank behind me, because I am the 82nd Airborne, and this is as far as the bastards are going!"

Policing is about "holding the line," much in the same way this paratrooper did, with pride, dedication, devotion, and an unwavering commitment to the mission you have chosen to carry out.

Every police officer says to the law-abiding community:

"Stand behind us—we will protect you. We will hold the line!"

Adapted from Dave Grossman's On Combat

Reportee Information
Address
Phone

15

HONORING *THE* CALL

It is disheartening *to think* that sometimes officers may not feel as though the work they go out into the streets daily to perform is a noble calling. When people are in need, and when others are unwilling to act, you are ready and prepared to serve and protect, no matter the call. Never— not even for a moment— doubt or underestimate your extraordinary role and the value of the path you have chosen. You have made a lifetime commitment willingly. It is a commitment that most dare not make, a sacrifice few are willing to shoulder, and a challenge only *the best* are capable of honoring!

Peggy Noonan wrote an article in *The Wall Street Journal* about the New York firefighters and police officers who lost their lives on September 11, 2001. She wrote:

"The men and women working in the towers were there that morning, and died. The firemen and rescue workers—they weren't there, they went there. They didn't run from the fire, they ran into the fire. They didn't run down the staircase, they ran up the staircase. **They didn't lose their lives, they gave them.** *"*

Few police officers will face the kind of danger that the heroes of September 11 encountered. But every man and woman who answers the call of policing understands that he or she lives facing ever-present uncertainty and risk.

You accept the risk because with that risk comes the opportunity to make a difference each and every day. Big or small matters not: **to touch a life today is the true reward.** Those are the priceless moments you will remember most. They are the "human" moments where you offer kindness and compassion, or a strong shoulder to lean on, or a confident hand to hold, or a willing heart to listen. It is in these smallest of moments where the mission of policing is realized. It is where Plato's vision becomes a reality, where the guardians honor a noble cause!

geographical boundaries of this town. The parking lot was full and the vehicle in here was enough room for emergency vehicles to pass with no obstructions.

WALKING THE

Lt. John Morrison of the San Diego Police Department wrote this letter to his officers who were in deep mourning after officers Harry Tiffany and Ron Ebeltoft were killed in the line of duty. His words speak to us all and are a powerful reminder of the ever-present risk and the unquestioned honor of our nation's finest!

POINT

All of us have heard by now the many versions of what happened on Crandell Street on a Saturday afternoon, and how we came to lose Officers Harry Tiffany and Ron Ebeltoft. Some of us even know the truth. And a few of us, apart from the table pounders and chronic fault seekers, know that there are some things you just can't do without suffering, very literally and profoundly, casualties—and our job is one of them!

You can't race cars without crashes, you can't dig mines without cave-ins, and you sure as hell can't send cops out into the streets of a violent society without violent deaths! Tiffany and Ebeltoft knew that, and they did it anyway—as we all do. Those who knew them well say that they did it because they loved it, and any of us who can't say that should envy them for it. At least they died doing what they loved to do, and that is something we can never explain to those outside our profession. You can't be a cop because you didn't get some other job. You can only be a cop because you want it!

There is an answer for why they died, something I learned half a world away, many years ago as a young soldier, preparing to face an enemy in combat for the first time. It was then that my sergeant explained that there are only three rules in war.

Rule 1: Young men die.

Rule 2: You can't change Rule 1.

Rule 3: Somebody's got to walk the point.

You see, when soldiers advance, knowing the enemy is near, there is always one man way out in front of everyone else. His duty is to look and listen, and sense that first contact. To spot the enemy, pinpoint an ambush, fire the first shot—and as a consequence, take those first shots. It offends the

logical mind and denies the instinct for survival. It ages and saddens and wizens—and sometimes kills those who take their turn walking the point! But it must be done, or there would be no protection for the rest; there would be more bloodshed, and more grief. The point man is there to save lives, even if he gives his own in the process.

Well, society isn't a company of soldiers, but it sure has somebody walking the point. Every time you go out the station-house door, every time you answer a radio call, every time you stop to check something suspicious—you can't change Rule 1!

If I could say something to the people of this city, it would be this: I know some of you will remember our two brothers—but that's not good enough. I want you to honor them for what they did for you—they certainly didn't have to do it. I'm not just talking about what they did on Saturday, June 6. That was a routine call that went horribly bad. I mean, what they did for you day after day, in darkness and light, rain or shine, without ever expecting even a thank-you. Tiffany and Ebeltoft volunteered to walk the point.

- **Honor them. Remember them. And in the quiet peace of your home, get down on you knees and thank God—that they volunteered to take your turn walking the point!**

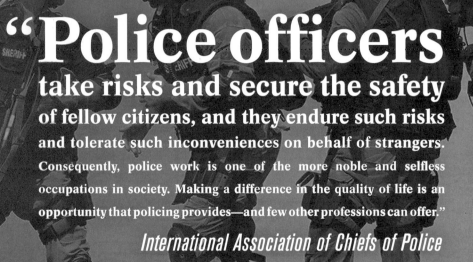

"Police officers

take risks and secure the safety

of fellow citizens, and they endure such risks and tolerate such inconveniences on behalf of strangers. Consequently, police work is one of the more noble and selfless occupations in society. Making a difference in the quality of life is an opportunity that policing provides—and few other professions can offer."

International Association of Chiefs of Police

THE NOBLE TRUTH

Critical Responsibilities

What makes policing such a noble calling?
Take a moment to think about the responsibilities of policing:

❏ *To preserve freedom and uphold democracy*
❏ *To uphold the law*
❏ *To ensure justice*
❏ *To protect life*
❏ *To keep the peace*

Rel. Info

*While the responsibilities of policing are great,
equally so are the tools given to police officers to carry
them out. These tools and accompanying power are
unlike that of any other existing profession, job, or craft.*

POWERFUL REALIT

*Within our borders, only the police have the
authority to use these powers to their fullest,
and at their sole discretion.*

24

KCMO

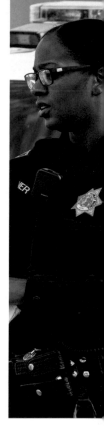

The Law

The law is the cornerstone of any democracy. It is an expression of principles with an aim at preserving the sanctity of a nation. A badge is a symbol of an officer's authority to enforce laws, but it is the person behind the badge who must exercise the judgment as to how the law is used.

The Use of Force

Police officers have the power and authority to use force, up to and including deadly force. Sadly, the headlines too often reflect or portray an incident where force was used too quickly, too strongly, with the wrong intent. The expectation in a democracy is that force will be used sparingly and only in those circumstances where it is lawful.

The Power of Incarceration

In a nation where our most precious gift is freedom, police officers can take that freedom away in an instant.

The tools a nation entrusts to the police are given with an expectation that those tools will be used as intended. As a hammer can tear down a structure built with care a hundred years ago, the powerful tools of policing can uphold or threaten the ideals of democracy that were shaped thousands of years ago.

NOBLE USE OF

POWER

"Nearly all men can stand adversity, but if you want to test a man's character, give him power."

Abraham Lincoln

Character is what guides every officer in those countless moments of truth and choice.

A philosopher once said:

"When people of action cease to believe in a cause, they then begin to believe only in the action."

It is so easy for a police officer to lose focus on the "cause" of policing—**service, justice, and fundamental fairness**—and begin to focus on the powerful call of the "action" the job brings.

27

MOTORCYCLE CHASE *Cause VS. Action*

I n the mid 1970s, my partner and I stopped a motorcyclist for a traffic violation. While we were writing the tickets, the violator was standing inside the open paddy-wagon door as we talked. Since the bike was one of the hottest and fastest on the market, we asked how fast it could really go. He replied, "Well, what would you do if I got on it and drove away?" Without a thought I replied, "I guess we'd see how fast your bike is, wouldn't we?" At that point he began to walk toward his bike.

Oddly enough, my partner and I simply watched him go without even a thought that we should stop him. In fact, at one point I said to my partner, "He's not going to do this, is he?" My partner replied, "I don't know," but as he was replying, he was putting the gearshift of our vehicle in drive, preparing to give chase.

The motorcyclist got on his bike, started it, and took off. The chase was on! We found ourselves chasing the fastest bike on the market, down the busiest street in our city—and we were in a paddy wagon! At no time did we think about service, justice, and fundamental fairness. At that point, it was all about the "action"—the thrill of a chase. And it was great fun, until the motorcycle crashed violently, flipping several times and severely injuring the violator.

Had we focused on the "cause" of policing that day, we would have never allowed him to get back on the bike—let alone flee. We certainly had the ability to stop him. We chose not to. In truth, I actually challenged him with my comment: "I guess we'd see how fast your bike is, wouldn't we?"

How often do we police officers challenge those we are sworn to serve? Sadly enough, there are many people in our communities—especially at times of low public trust—who are up for taking on those challenges.

I learned that day that there are consequences for all my words, actions, and even inaction—and that a police officer's focus must be on the "cause," not the "action."

There is always plenty of action without our creating it!

THE POWER OF
influence

char•ac•ter |ˈkarəktə(r)|

Your personal maturity, integrity, and principles—who and what you are.

Public approval depends on a relationship of trust between the police and the community." Trust only flows from "trustworthiness," which is a combination of character (who you are) and competence (your ability to do your job). For a police officer, neither can stand alone. They are twin pillars that allow others to trust your intentions, directions, and influence.

When the ability to influence through your professionalism, demeanor, integrity, and confidence is absent, you are forced to rely on the tools of power to get the job done. You are forced to use a stick—the law—or other forceful means to gain compliance.

Being trustworthy makes your work easier and safer! You then become a person of influence who is backed by power when it is necessary.

30

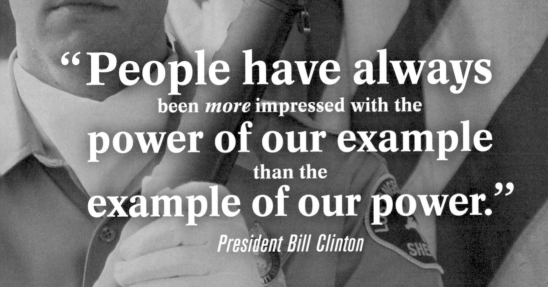

"**People have always** been *more* impressed with the **power of our example** than the **example of our power.**"

President Bill Clinton

"Our profession must hire **convincingly *good* people.** The communities we serve **deserve *no less.*** "

Sheriff Lee Baca,
Los Angeles County, California

THE IMPORTANCE OF Character

An FBI agent turns spy, a police officer goes to prison for corruption, a citizen loses a loved one due to a delayed response, parents cannot let their child play outside after dark because of an unsafe neighborhood...

"Those who are here unfaithfully do incredible damage."

Jalal ad-Din Rumi

A giant redwood is among the most majestic and beautiful trees on Earth. But how do they grow to such impressive heights? How have they earned such admiration and respect by anyone who looks upon them?

These giants stand upon a firm foundation—strong, interconnected roots. While we admire the majesty of what is above the ground, it is the unseen roots that provide the strength to withstand the forces of time and nature. A police officer's foundation is his or her character—what is beneath the surface—that provides the armor that protects the soul, ensures justice, and preserves a nation.

The good character of the men and women who take the oath are the roots upon which great policing is built. Demonstrating character, especially in times of great challenge, reflects the honor and nobility of the profession.

• *The character of every officer has the ability to damage and degrade, or nourish and strengthen, this vital foundation.*

"Every action we take, every interaction with a citizen, every moment we're visible is a commercial for our profession."

Terry Hillard, former Superintendent of the Chicago Police Department

"It's 3 a.m.

I am on patrol, alone in a police car. My only company is the endless chatter on the radio. The streets are quiet and the houses I pass are dark. It is in moments like this that I realize what policing is truly about. **The community sleeps** in the quiet and comfort and safety of their homes because I am out here. I am awake, vigilant, ready, and prepared to protect and serve. The city sleeps and reenergizes itself for a new day while **I work to keep it safe.** As the dawn approaches, the houses begin to light up, and the city **awakes** and prepares for a new day. While the city works, I will sleep, renew, and prepare to guard it once again."

The Core ······················
PRINCIPLES
of Policing
Service, Justice, and Fundamental Fairness

When you honor these principles and stay true to the promise you made—the oath—you can predict with some certainty the results. When you choose your actions based on your values and principles, you exercise control over the events and direction of your life.

This is the bold act of doing what is right despite the consequences. It is the bold act of embracing humanity and treating those less fortunate than yourself with the dignity and respect they deserve. It is the bold act of living your life with a balance that honors not just your work, but your relationships and all of your commitments.

- *While everyone and everything around you is in turmoil, the constants are your principles. Honor them and they will guide you to the right place.*

38

Thoughts become words.
Words become actions.
Actions **become** habits.
Habits become character.
Character becomes **destiny.**

—Unknown

> # "A principle
> ## is a principle, and in no case
> ### can it be watered down because of our
> incapacity to live it in practice. We have to strive to
> achieve it, and the striving should be conscious, deliberate, and hard."
>
> *Mahatma Gandhi*

UNIFORM CITATION AND COMPLAINT

Use for All Violations or Crimes Where Separate Complaint Will Not Be Filed/ORS 153.045 or 133.069

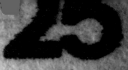

भारत
INDIA

गांधीजी GANDHIJI

41

BEING FIT:

BODY, HEART, MIND, AND SPIRIT

If you choose law enforcement, you lose the right to be unfit.

Banner hanging in the Illinois State Police Academy

Being ready and prepared is about being "fit" in a way that is so much more than just physical. It means keeping your mind, heart, and spirit in peak readiness to answer the call. As a whole person, you must remain fit in all areas to maximize your effectiveness.

When you commit to renew yourself on a regular basis in each of these four areas of life, you become more effective in every part of your life. In this way, you take care of policing's most important asset—you.

Body

This is your physical well-being. You build physical wellness through exercise, nutrition, rest, and stress management.

Mind

This involves a constant quest for learning. You increase your mental capacity by reading, writing, continuously learning, and being endlessly curious.

Heart

This is about nurturing all the relationships in your life. You become stronger socially and emotionally by building strong and lasting relationships with family, friends, co-workers, and members of the community, and by showing compassion, fairness, and justice.

Spirit

This is about YOU—your sense of self. You develop spirituality by reflection, journaling, performing service, spending time in nature, showing respect, having the passion to make a difference, and performing random acts of kindness.

The term "unfit"
has a deeper meaning...
to be unfit means to be incapable or unsuitable.

It applies to the state of mind, along with the physical state. A police officer gives up the right to be immoral and unjust, and the responsibility that befalls an officer wearing a badge is one that requires mental aptitude and superior skill in problem solving. *Being "fit" means acting within the scope of our authority and with fundamental fairness in mind. It means putting our personal views aside and acting within the parameters of the law without prejudice and bias.*

Article by Cdr. Kristen Ziman, Aurora, IL, Police Department published in The Beacon News.

RAILROAD P

0183

A REMINDER:

Why is policing an honorable and noble profession? Because you are the frontline protectors of democracy, you promote freedom and justice every day, and you preserve the integrity of the law you have sworn to protect.

365 days a year, 24/7, rain or shine, the police are there—you never close the station-house doors!

What you do every moment of every day touches lives.

This is the profession to which you have dedicated your life and the reason why you and your family make the sacrifices that you do daily.

STOP &

"When you begin to doubt the nobility of your mission or the sanctity of your profession because your heart is heavy, or you feel anger, disillusionment, disenfranchisement, betrayed, or confused—stop and listen to the voices…the voices that rise up…from a field in Pennsylvania, from a wall at the Pentagon, and from the spot of the Earth the world has come to know as Ground Zero.

0326

LISTEN

Because if you listen, you will hear those souls tell you 'thank you' for what you do…hear them cheering you on. Let them carry you through this difficult moment, allow them to nourish you and encourage you, and doubt no more, for you are warriors and champions for those who have gone before and to those most vulnerable now. *You are admired and respected, for you are the best at what you do."*

John R. Thomas, Former First Deputy Superintendent of the Chicago Police Department

THE NATURE OF "FAILURE"

A sea turtle lays hundreds of eggs and buries them deep in the sand. In reality, very few eggs will survive. But those that do will grow, mature, and eventually repeat the cycle, allowing the species to flourish over time. For that reason, the effort is a success.

It is true that many good deeds go unnoticed, unrewarded, and even challenged by the people you are serving. But these are not failures or a sign the cause is lost. Every just and noble act is an opportunity to make a positive difference. Every one of those moments matters in service to a greater good.

YOUR ACTIONS ALWAYS MATTER TO SOMEONE

O nce upon a time, there was a wise man who would go to the ocean to do his writing. He had a habit of walking on the beach before he began his work. One day, as he was walking along the shore, he looked down the beach and saw a human figure moving like a dancer. As he got closer, he noticed that the figure was that of a young man, and that he was not dancing at all. The young man was reaching down, picking up small objects, and throwing them into the ocean.

He came closer still and called out, *"Good morning! May I ask what it is that you are doing?"*

The young man replied, *"Throwing starfish into the ocean."*

"I must ask, then, why are you throwing starfish into the ocean?" said the somewhat startled wise man.

To this, the young man replied, *"The sun is up and the tide is going out. If I don't throw them in, they'll die."*

Upon hearing this, the wise man commented, *"But, young man, do you not realize that there are miles and miles of beach and there are starfish along every mile? You can't possibly make a difference!"*

At this, the young man bent down, picked up yet another starfish, and threw it into the ocean. As it met the water, he said, *"It made a difference for that one."*

Adapted from The Star Thrower *by Loren Eiseley*

REMAINING faithful

BEING STRONG IN THE HARD MOMENTS

Ultimately, the nobility of policing is **a choice** to be made by every police officer. Each day you must decide what kind of police officer you will be. The endless moments of truth and choice that you face will make all the difference in determining who and what you are. It is a personal choice—to adhere to your principles through the job stress, an unforgiving media, conflict with the community, and challenges and changes to the profession that are beyond your control. To be strong in the hard moments is the most difficult of all challenges, and it is why you have been chosen!

Throughout constant change, remember the ever-present need. The people and communities you serve will always depend on you. Your presence gives comfort to those you protect, because you are always there.

• **Without you, the consequences would be unthinkable.**

Policing is MO

- ❏ **Caring** more than others think is wise.
- ❏ **Risking** more than others think is safe.
- ❏ **Believing** more than others think is practical.
- ❏ **Expecting** more than others think is possible.

18063

On September 4, 2012,

California Highway Patrol Officer Kenyon Youngstrom, #18063, was parked on the right shoulder of I-680 near Alamo when his partner, Officer Tyler Carlton, #19662, advised over the radio that he intended to initiate a traffic stop on a Jeep for an obstructed license plate. Officer Youngstrom stepped out of his cruiser to direct the Jeep to the side of the road, just as Officer Carlton pulled his cruiser in behind the Jeep. Officer Youngstrom approached the driver of the Jeep from the front of the driver's side when the driver fired a gun, hitting Youngstrom. Moments later, Officer Carlton approached the Jeep from the rear passenger side, returned fire and killed the gunman. Officer Youngstrom succumbed to his injuries on September 5, 2012. Officer Youngstrom was 37 years of age, a seven-year CHP veteran officer, and a father to four children.

Never doubt that you carry a message of hope wherever you go.
For the people you influence, protect, and serve, that you may never meet.
For every right thought, word, deed, and action that serves the cause.
For what you have done yesterday, today, and will do tomorrow
to honor the nobility of policing.

Thank you.

21,514
UNITED STATES & CANADA

Throughout the pages of this book, there are numbers that represent
the fallen law enforcement heroes in both the United States and
Canada*. Our thoughts and prayers are with their loved ones.

*As of September 2011. Per The Officer Down Memorial Page, Inc. (www.odmp.org and www.odmp.org/canada/)

FranklinCovey's Law Enforcement Services helps organizations succeed by creating leaders at all levels of the organization and by helping them focus and execute on top priorities, all while tailoring this message to the unique needs of law enforcement professionals. Clients include federal, state, and local agencies throughout the United States, Canada, and the world. Organizations and individuals access FranklinCovey products and services through on-site training, licensed client facilitators, one-on-one coaching, public workshops, and **www.franklincovey.com/lawenforcement.**

Dr. Stephen R. Covey, an internationally respected leadership expert, is the author of several acclaimed books, including The *7 Habits of Highly Effective People.* This *New York Times* #1 international bestseller has also been on the bestseller lists of *Business Week, USA Today,* and *Publishers Weekly* for more than five years. Sales of this powerful book exceed 15 million, in 28 languages and 70 countries worldwide.

Michael Nila is a retired Police Commander from Aurora, Illinois, where he served for 29 years. He is recognized as one of the nation's foremost authorities in the practices of great leaders and organizations. His mission is to inspire individuals and teams to achieve their highest potential. A valued, sought-after speaker, Michael travels extensively to deliver his trademark real-world perspective to contemporary issues in both the public and private sectors.

Michael has dedicated his career to his uncle, Hector Jordan, Aurora's first minority police officer, hired in 1955. Hector Jordan became a U.S. Federal Narcotics Agent and lost his life in the line of duty in 1970. It was from his uncle that Michael first learned the nobility of policing.

We would like to extend a special thanks to the following individuals and organizations for allowing us to include their stories, quotes, and photos to tell this important story of the nobility of policing.

Sheriff Lee Baca—Los Angeles County Sheriff's Department

Edward Corral Photography

Delaware State Police

Cynthia Gonzales—City of Aurora

Superintendant Terry Hillard (Ret.)—Chicago Police Department

Kevin Jenkins—Aurora Police Department

Kansas City (MO) Police Department

Los Angeles County Sheriff's Department

The Family of Deputy David March—Los Angeles County Sheriff's Department

Miami Beach Police Department

Lt. John Morrison—San Diego Police Department

Kristina Ripatti—Los Angeles Police Department

Former First Deputy Superintendant John Thomas—Chicago Police Department

Cdr. Kristin Ziman—Aurora Police Department